# BOOK ANALYSIS

By Anna Savory

# The Ballad of Reading Gaol

## BY OSCAR WILDE

# OSCAR WILDE

- **Born in Dublin in 1854.**
- **Died in Paris in 1900.**
- **Notable works:**
  - *The Picture of Dorian Gray* (1890), novel
  - *The Importance of Being Earnest* (1895), play
  - *An Ideal Husband* (1899), play

Oscar Wilde was born in Dublin to Anglo-Irish parents. He moved to England in 1874 to study at Oxford University, where his tutors included Walter Pater (English essayist, 1839-1894) and John Ruskin (English art critic, 1819-1900). Through them, Wilde became interested in the philosophy of aestheticism, or 'art for art's sake'. After university he moved to London, where he became a leading figure in high society known for his decadence, fashion and wit. He wrote numerous plays and poems during this period and toured the USA giving lectures on aestheticism. In 1884, he married Constance Lloyd (1859-1898), though he had many relationships with men during their marriage, including Robert Ross (Canadian journalist, 1869-1918) and Wilde's great love Lord Alfred 'Bosie' Douglas (British writer, 1870-1945). In 1895, he was arrested on charges of 'gross indecency' (homosexuality) and sentenced to two years in Reading Gaol. He was released in 1897. With his reputation in tatters he moved to Paris, where he lived in poverty until his death in 1900.

# *THE BALLAD OF READING GAOL*

## WILDE'S INDICTMENT OF CAPITAL PUNISHMENT

- **Genre:** poem
- **Reference edition:** Wilde, O. (2010) *The Ballad of Reading Gaol and Other Poems*. London: Penguin.
- **1st edition:** 1898
- **Themes:** the penal system, the death penalty, religion, sacrifice, punishment, guilt, love, justice, forgiveness

*The Ballad of Reading Gaol* was written in 1897 during Wilde's self-imposed exile in France. Wilde was released from Reading Gaol in May of that year and the poem draws strongly on his experiences there, specifically the hanging of fellow prisoner Charles Thomas Wooldridge (English soldier, 1866-1896) which had a great effect on Wilde. The poem was published by Leonard Smithers (English publisher, 1861-1907) in 1898. Since Wilde's name was already infamous in England and would have damaged the critical reception of the work and the reputation of the publisher, *The Ballad of Reading Gaol* was published under Wilde's prison number C.3.3. (his cell was in cell block C, on the 3$^{rd}$ floor, and was the 3$^{rd}$ cell from the left). Despite some critics feeling that the poem's political message (a rallying cry against capital punishment and in favour of penal reform) overshadowed its aesthetic achievements, it was a success with the general public. It enjoyed six additional print runs in its first year, with Wilde's name added in square brackets next to C.3.3. for the sixth edition. The poem provided Wilde with a small income upon which he depended for the remaining three years of his life.

# SUMMARY

## CANTO I

The poem opens with a description by the narrator (an authorial stand-in; for all intents and purposes indistinguishable from Wilde) of a fellow prisoner, a soldier, who, while not named, is generally assumed to be based on Charles Thomas Wooldridge to whom the poem is dedicated. Wooldridge was Wilde's fellow inmate and was executed at Reading Gaol in 1896. The poem's narrator details the soldier's manner of dress (he has eschewed his red military uniform, which carries unfortunate associations with blood and wine, in favour of a grey suit), and reveals that he is in prison for killing his wife. The narrator watches the soldier looking "wistfully at the sky" (p. 3) in the exercise yard, and is told by other inmates that he is going to be hanged. Upset by the news, he muses on the nature of guilt and crime, and presents one of the poem's central conceits: that "each man kills the thing he loves" (p. 4) and that it is unfair that the soldier alone will be punished for a crime that all are guilty of. The narrator lists what the soldier will experience in the run-up to his execution: being watched in his cell the night before to check that he will not kill himself; being collected by the prison's chaplain and doctor; having to listening to the Burial Office read; being led to the gallows, and so on. He stresses that other equally guilty people (both prisoners and humanity as a whole) will not have to endure these things.

## CANTO 2

The narrator continues to watch the soldier in the exercise yard in the six weeks leading up to his execution. The narrator and his fellow prisoners regard him with awe because he is "light and gay" (p. 6) despite his imminent execution (though he does still look at the sky wistfully). The narrator reflects on this, presenting contrasting images of happiness and doom ("the oak and elm have pleasant leaves [...] but grim to see is the gallows tree", p. 7; "it is sweet to dance to violins [...] but it is not sweet with nimble feet/ to dance upon the air", p. 8). Eventually the soldier stops coming to the exercise yard, and the narrator knows that he has been called to the dock to receive his final sentence and that he will not see him alive again. He reflects upon their time together and how, despite not speaking to each other or making any sort of contact, they shared an intrinsic bond because they were both "thrust" from "the world's heart" and from "out God's care" (p. 9).

## CANTO 3

The narrator (who often functions less as a literal character and more as an omnipotent presence) details what is happening to the soldier in the run-up to his execution (a deliberate mirroring of and expansion upon the earlier list in Canto 1): he is watched by guards, day and night, to ensure that he does not kill himself; he is visited by the prison administrators, Governor, Doctor and Chaplain, and so on. The narrator describes how, in spite of his situation, the soldier is "resolute" (p. 10), unafraid, and often wishes that the execution would come sooner. It is implied that the prison Warder would like to know why this is but cannot ask in case it compromises his professionalism and he is "moved [...] to comfort and console" (*ibid*.). Instead he must "make his face a mask" (*ibid.*) and engage with the soldier only as a prisoner and not as a human being.

The narrator shifts focus back to the other prisoners, and describes their labour routine, including the daily "slouch and swing" (*ibid.*) around the exercise yard; picking oakum (a common punishment at the time); cleaning; mending; breaking stones and so on, and notes how, even while engaged in these tasks, "terror lies still" (p. 11) in the hearts of the prisoners.

The narrator, returning from hard labour, passes a freshly dug grave in the prison yard and he and the other inmates realise the soldier will be hung tomorrow. They experience a collective guilt and fear ("through each brain on hands of pain/ another's terror crept" (p. 12) on behalf of the soldier, who himself sleeps soundly in his cell. The narrator describes the long night before the execution during which the other prisoners all uncharacteristically pray, and are haunted by visions of "evil sprites" and "phantoms" (p. 14) which dance through the gaol taunting them with their own crimes. Despite feeling that morning will never come, the narrator describes a slow red dawn, and how he and the other inmates spend the early morning in a collective mood of hopelessness, waiting for eight o'clock, when they know the execution will take place. When eight o'clock is "smote on the shivering air" (p. 17) by the prison clock, the inmates have a collective vision of the hanging and cry out on the soldiers behalf, as if suffering with him. The narrator notes this communal suffering, and reaffirms the link between the soldier and him specifically, stating that no-one knows the soldier's regrets and pains as well as he does.

## CANTO 4

The fourth canto opens with the narrator stating that there is no church service on the day of a hanging because the prison Chaplain is both exhausted and spiritually tainted by having been so close to enforced death. The narrator notes that every other prisoner in the yard is ashen-faced and deeply affected by what has happened, and that as they walk round and round each man is reflecting on his own crimes and how he also deserves execution. The narrator notes that the Warders' manners are unchanged, and that they go about their duties unperturbed. He states that while one would not know from looking at their neat uniforms that there has been an execution, he suspects they have been burying the dead soldier because of the quicklime (a chemical compound used to speed decomposition) on their shoes.

This suspicion is confirmed when the narrator reaches the prison wall and finds that the grave that was open yesterday has now been filled. He imagines the quicklime eating away at the soldier's bones and heart, and states that the warders will not plant anything as a marker on the grave for fear that "each simple seed they sowed" (p. 20) would be tainted by the moral corruption of the soldier. The narrator, however, theorises that any plant growing from the grave would thrive and bloom beautifully and reflects on how it would be a symbol of Christ's redemptive power as well as an aesthetic comfort to the other prisoners if they would plant a red and white rose on the gravesite.

He reflects on the disrespectful and unchristian way that the soldier's body has been treated (hanged "as a beast is hanged", p. 21; not given a requiem; mocked by the warders when dead; and buried in an unmarked grave on unconsecrated ground) but concludes that he is at peace (or at least will be soon) and that he will be mourned, not only by the prisoners but by all outcast men, a mourning all the more pointed and effective because "outcasts always mourn" (p. 22).

## CANTO 5

The fifth canto moves away from the established narrative and instead uses the religious themes touched upon in earlier cantos as the basis of a larger treatise on the flaws of the penal system. The narrator stresses that while he cannot comment on whether the law itself is just, gaols, as institutions, are inherently unjust and brutal. He notes that prisons are built with high walls and barred windows not only so that the occupants cannot see out, but so that humanity and God cannot see in, and that far from being reformed or improved by gaol, all that is good within the inmates dies there. He details the poor physical as well as poor spiritual conditions, noting the "brackish water" and "bitter bread" (p. 24) given as rations, and particularly the mental toll that hard labour takes on prisoners: "what chills and kills outright/ is that every stone one lifts by day/ becomes one's heart by night" (*ibid.*). While he condemns humanity for having created this sort of system, the narrator notes that the terrible suffering undergone by prisoners wins them spiritual redemption and God's love and concludes by stating that the soul of the dead soldier will be welcomed into heaven.

## CANTO 6

The sixth canto is the poem's shortest and acts as a conclusion. Repeating lines and motifs from the earlier cantos, the narrator presents the image of the soldier's grave beside Reading Gaol, reflects on the second coming of Christ, and repeats the poem's central paradox that "each man kills the thing he loves" (p. 4).

# CHARACTER STUDY

## THE NARRATOR

The figure of the narrator is heavily based upon, and in many ways indistinguishable from, Wilde himself, who spent two years in Reading Gaol in the late 1890s. The allusions to classicism and aestheticism, and the biblical references throughout the poem imply that, like Wilde, the Narrator is an educated aesthete and a (possibly lapsed) Catholic. We are never told what crime the narrator has committed (although we do know he is guilty of some permutation of the universal crime: killing the thing he loves most). The Narrator feels an intimate connection with his condemned fellow-prisoner the Soldier whom he views as sympathetic and noble.

## THE SOLDIER

Just as the figure of the Narrator is for all intents and purposes indistinguishable from Wilde, the Soldier is a thinly veiled portrait of Charles Thomas Wooldridge, a former member of the

Royal Horse Guards and convicted murderer whom Wilde met during his time in Reading Gaol. Unlike the Narrator's crimes, the Soldier's crime is explicitly stated in the poem's opening stanza: he has murdered his wife and in doing so "kill[ed] the thing he loves" (p. 4). Wilde implies that this specific crime represents and embodies a universal crime ("each man kills the thing he loves", *ibid*.) and that in being hanged for murder the Soldier is, in effect, suffering on behalf of an equally guilty society.

## THE WARDER

The Warder is employed by the gaol to guard the prisoners, both in their cells and while in the exercise yard. He is referred to at several points in the ballad, most notably in Canto 2 when Wilde highlights the need for the Warder to suppress his natural urge to interact with the condemned in case he begins to humanise them and is moved to "comfort and console'" (p. 10). The fact that the suppression of compassion and humanity is necessary to allow the institution to function is a key point in Wilde's indictment of the penal system. It is not clear whether Wilde is referring to different Warders or the same Warder at various points in the ballad, and in many respects it is not important. The figure of the Warder is a stand-in for all Warders and for the concept of authority more generally. It is worth noting that many of the supporting characters in *The Ballad of Reading Gaol* have this in common: they lack distinct personal characters but rather function as penal or societal archetypes.

## THE CHAPLAIN

The Chaplain is the gaol's religious leader and is employed to provide prisoners with spiritual guidance and council. Although *The Ballad of Reading Gaol* is inherently religious in tone, Wilde presents a fairly negative portrait of the Chaplain, whose "little tracts" (p. 10) and sermons are simply a matter of routine and provide no real comfort. The Chaplain is, himself, spiritually corrupted by having to attend hangings, and, broadly, represents Christianity as a flawed institution, not as a personal redemptive experience.

# THE GOVERNOR

The Governor is the ultimate authority within the gaol and therefore the embodiment of authority and punishment in the most general sense. A forbidding character, his appearance is dehumanised and Death-like; he is a "dread figure" dressed "all in shiny black, with the yellow face of Doom" (p. 5). While his physical descriptions evoke images of final, divine judgement, the actual judgement he doles out is inherently human, i.e. not divine judgement (which Wilde implies would be marked by forgiveness and grace) but the flawed and unforgiving judgement of the penal system.

# ANALYSIS

## RELIGION AND RELIGIOUS IMAGERY

Religion looms large throughout *The Ballad of Reading Gaol*, both in terms of explicit textual references and implicit allusions. Perhaps the most striking example of the latter is the obvious and continued equation of the Soldier with the figure of Christ. From his introduction in the first stanza, the Soldier is deliberately reminiscent of Jesus: simultaneously debased and noble; calm and beatific in the face of death; and in the process of being punished by a misguided and unforgiving state authority. It is no coincidence that the Narrator exclaims "Dear Christ!" (p. 3; at once an oath, an invocation, and an oblique comparison) upon discovering that the Soldier is going to be hanged. The distinctly redemptive framing of the Soldier's execution only adds to this. In paying the ultimate price for a crime which Wilde asserts everyone is guilty of, the Soldier's death becomes an act of symbolic significance that invites comparisons with the crucifixion (it is worth noting that there is something distinctly Roman in the laughter and mockery of the Warders as they stand over the Soldier's body).

Wilde makes it is clear, however, that the Soldier is only Christ-like, and not a stand in for Christ Himself (who is referenced and invoked in His own right on numerous occasions throughout the poem), as for all his paralleled holiness the Soldier is still a murderer (found with literal blood on his hands) who must do penance, in both the religious and the secular sense, in Reading Gaol. The Soldier, therefore, is a dual figure, at once pure and corrupt (neatly symbolised by the red and white roses that the narrator imagines growing from his grave) and his religious connotations are two-fold: he is both redemptive, and suffering in order to earn his own redemption.

The latter is true for all the prisoners, and while Wilde rails against the inhumane physical demands of hard labour, the sense of Catholic penance it carries with it is spiritually fitting. For the Narrator, at least, it is only through physical suffering that prisoners can "cleanse themselves of sin" (p. 14) and win forgiveness. Although this conflates slightly the divine judgement of God with the unforgiving judgements of the penal system, Wilde is careful to draw a distinction between the two; indeed, they are set in ironic opposition to each other throughout the poem, and the Narrator reminds us that "God's eternal laws are kind" (p. 20) and forgiving, while the laws of man are anything but.

As well as a generally religious tone, *The Ballad of Reading Gaol* also abounds with specific textual references to religion which further enforce the gulf between divine judgement and the judgement of the state: the priest Caiaphas is referenced, as is the biblical motif of the crowing cock ("the grey cock crew, the red cock crew", p. 12) and the "rings" that the "souls in pain" (p. 3) walk in the exercise yard are deliberately reminiscent of the circles of Hell. It is notable that the first biblical image we encounter is the fruit-bearing "spring-time" (p. 7) tree of the first canto, and the last, in the final canto, is Christ "call[ing] forth the dead" (p. 26) for the rapture, meaning that Wilde effectively takes us from Genesis to Revelations over the course of the ballad. Even the poem's most famous stanza...

> "But each man kills the thing he loves,
> By all let this be heard,
> Some do it with a bitter look,
> Some with a flattering word,
> The coward does it with a kiss,
> The brave man with a sword." (p. 4)

...is not without a subtle nod towards the biblical. 'The coward does it with a kiss' is a reference to Judas' betrayal of Christ in Gethsemane (although it also has a second, more secular meaning: an allusion to taboo love and Wilde's current situation).

Religion, therefore, is at the heart of *The Ballad of Reading Gaol* both textually and thematically and its primary function is to highlight the injustice of the penal system by setting harsh punishment and judgement against divine forgiveness and grace. Wilde loved a paradox in his poetry as much as in his bon mots and it would not have been lost on him or his readers that, while the judicial and penal system was predicated on strictly Christian moral values, its lack of forgiveness and compassion flew directly in the face of Christ's teachings. It is the prisoners, sincere and tragic in their penitence, that come out of the poem, if not Christ-like, then at least washed clean by the 'tears of Christ', while the supposedly morally upstanding and exacting penal system is an offence both to man and God.

## THE FUNCTION OF FORM: WHY WILDE CHOSE A BALLAD

In order to fully understand the function of form in *The Ballad of Reading Gaol* it is important to first look at the ballad and its connotations in a wider historical context.

Ballads are one of the oldest traditional poetic forms, dating back to the late medieval period. Usually comprised of alternating 8- and 6-syllable lines, with a similarly alternating rhyme scheme and numerous repeating refrains, ballads were originally intended to be set to music and sung by minstrels. The effect of this was that they could be enjoyed by a largely illiterate population who had no previous access to poetry, and as a result the form itself quickly became synonymous with the working classes. Unlike later Italianate forms (i.e. sonnets, villanelles, etc.), ballads were marked by an emphasis on narrative story telling over poetic finesse and traditional themes included heroics, high adventure, chivalry and love affairs.

Given Wilde's background as a high-society aesthete, his use of a historically rough-and-ready, proletarian form is in some ways surprising, though there is no question that it was a deliberate choice. There are several notable effects that the use of the form produces. On a purely metrical level its plodding iambic tetrameter and characteristically balladic refrains mirror the relentless, repetitive routine of hard labour. More generally speaking there are faint socialist connotations in using a form associated with the working classes (which compliments the left-leaning politics of the piece as a whole). The dichotomy between form and content can even be read as a microcosm of Wilde's experience in prison: rarefied, beautiful reflections hemmed in by a base and arguably debasing poetic form.

Notably, though, Wilde seemed aware that in appealing to popular tastes with a ballad, he would further the reach of his political message and gain a new, thematically-apt audience, and also seems aware that the form may be apt in other ways. Wilde himself suggested that the poem be published in *Reynold's Magazine* "because it circulates widely among the criminal classes to which I now belong [...] at last I will be read by my peers, a new experience for me" (Kiberd, 2000: 336). At first glance, this statement reads like a typical Wildean aphorism (the implication being that when he was writing for high-society audiences he was peerless, i.e. unrivalled as a dramatist), but it is also a very real reflection on his relationship with the class system. The readers of *Reynold's Magazine* were his peers, not just because of his recent conviction, but in a deeper sense. For all that he had assimilated into English society and grown into the archetype of the English dandy, Wilde was originally a working-class colonial Irishman, synonymous in the public imagination with poverty and criminality, for whom the oral tradition of the ballad form may well have held lingering cultural and social significance.

Finally, it is important to note another key effect that the use of the ballad produces. For all that the form carried working-class connotations, the subjects of traditional ballads were rarely the disenfranchised poor who read or listened to them; on the contrary, ballads were reserved for tales of heroes and knights, chivalric figures engaged in adventure and action. In employing a form traditionally associated (in terms of subject, if not reader) with nobility, bravery, and glory to write about criminals, Wilde both draws an ironic distinction and invites a comparison. He contrasts the two, but in doing so elevates the latter. There is a gulf between the prisoners and traditional ballad heroes, but in a way the residents of Reading Gaol are just as valid, just as brave, just as worthy of the balladry as Arthurian knights or Robin Hood. Perhaps the most powerful effect of the ballad form as employed in *The Ballad of Reading Gaol*, then, is that it elevates the figures at its heart and imbues them with an importance, heroism, and dignity that itself sits in contrast with their current situation.

## TEXT IN CONTEXT: THE LATE VICTORIAN PENAL SYSTEM

Many contemporary critics felt that *The Ballad of Reading Gaol* was hampered poetically by what it was trying to achieve politically, and Wilde himself claimed it "suffered under the difficulty of a divided aim [...] part poetry and part propaganda" (Wilde, 1962: 654). For modern readers this seems like an arbitrary notion of what is or is not a proper subject for art, but regardless of whether or not its agenda compromised its aesthetics, it is certainly difficult to fully appreciate *The Ballad of Reading Gaol* without some knowledge of the political context in which it was written.

The mid-19th century saw a crisis in the British penal system when, with a steadily increasing crime rate at home, several colonies simultaneously refused to accept British convicts. Transportation had to be rapidly phased out, and sentences converted to incarceration and hard labour. The sudden demand for prisons to house this new and growing convict population lead to a wave of provincial gaols being built (of which Reading was one) as well as decommissioned warships being converted into the dreaded Thames prison hulks. Even with these new measures in place, the prison system was still in crisis and chronic overcrowding lead to unsanitary and often life-threatening conditions.

By the close of the century the crisis was beginning to ease, but prison conditions had not improved accordingly; moreover, new types of physical (hard) labour had been introduced, including breaking rocks, walking in wheels, and picking oakum (untangling old pieces of rope). Under the Assistant Director of Prisons Sir Edmund du Cane (1830-1903), conditions became even more extreme and harsh measures were justified by the popular belief that the purpose of prison was to punish and deter.

A subtle swing in public opinion occurred in the 1890s, however. Shocked by the increasingly harsh conditions, and having already lost their appetite for public executions (due in no small part to the efforts of another literary figure, Charles Dickens [English writer and social activist, 1812-1870], whose letter to *The Times* in 1849 denouncing the practice was instrumental getting it banned) Victorian society began to question the larger purpose of incarceration, what caused criminality and whether it was possible to be born bad. Many late Victorians began to subscribe to the view that prisons should primarily seek to reform and rehabilitate their inmates, and that harsh conditions only served to compound criminal impulses (these schools of thought would become more fully realised and start influencing public policy in the mid-Edwardian era, with the introduction of Reformatory Prisons or borstals for young offenders).

By the time Wilde's indictment of Reading Gaol was published, then, the tides were already starting to turn against capital punishment and the prison system as a whole. With this in mind, it is not difficult to imagine that the accusations levelled at the piece by conservative critics may have been motivated less by aesthetic ideals of what poetry ought to be, and more by an awareness of the potential that a passionate, first-hand account of prison life had to sway an already wavering public opinion.

# FURTHER REFLECTION

## SOME QUESTIONS TO THINK ABOUT...

- Consider the theme of forgiveness. What character(s) in the poem deserve forgiveness the most, and why?
- Many Victorian critics felt *The Ballad of Reading Gaol*'s political message interfered with its artistic value on the grounds that literature (especially poetry) should address timeless themes rather than contemporary issues. To what extent do you agree? Can and should literature have an overt political agenda? Is it possible for a poem to be both timeless and of its time?
- Consider dehumanisation in the poem. In what ways are the prisoners dehumanised by their experience? Also consider the figures of the Chaplain, Warders, and other representatives of the gaol itself. How are they are dehumanised by Wilde? Are there any ways in which he humanises them?

- To what extent do you agree with the assertion that *The Ballad of Reading Gaol*'s characters are more archetypes than individuals?

- Taking into account Wilde's lifelong devotion to aestheticism, look at the use of colour in *The Ballad of Reading Gaol*. What colours are referenced and to what effect?

- While the events described in *The Ballad of Reading Gaol* are autobiographical, and many of its characters are drawn directly from life, it is also full of classical, religious and fantastical imagery. Wilde described the poem as "a mixture of realism and romanticism"; which of these is more prominent?

- The meaning of the poem's famous refrain "each man kills the thing he loves" (p. 4) has been hotly debated since its publication. How do you interpret the line? (You might consider both literal and metaphorical death, betrayal, and the power of love to alter and corrupt its object in your answer).

- Compare *The Ballad of Reading Gaol* to Rudyard Kipling's (English novelist and poet, 1865-1936) *Barrack-Room Ballads* (1892); how is the traditional form employed and subverted by both poets?

*We want to hear from you!*
*Leave a comment on your online library*
*and share your favourite books on social media!*

# FURTHER READING

## REFERENCE EDITION

- Wilde, O. (2010) *The Ballad of Reading Gaol and Other Poems*. London: Penguin.

## REFERENCE STUDIES

- Kiberd, D. (2000) *Irish Classics*. London: Granta.
- Wilde, O. (1962) *The Letters of Oscar Wilde*. R. Hart-Davis, ed. New York: Harcourt, Brace & World, Inc.

## ADDITIONAL SOURCES

- Holland, M. (2003) *Irish Peacock and Scarlet Marquess: The Real Trial of Oscar Wilde*. London: Fourth Estate.
- May, T. (2006) *Victorian and Edwardian Prisons*. London: Bloomsbury.
- Strand, M. (2001) *The Making of A Poem: A Norton Anthology of Poetic Form*. London: W. W. Norton and Company.

## MORE FROM BRIGHTSUMMARIES.COM

- Reading guide – *An Ideal Husband* by Oscar Wilde.

- Reading guide – *Lady Windermere's Fan* by Oscar Wilde.

- Reading guide – *The Canterville Ghost* by Oscar Wilde.

- Reading guide – *The Importance of Being Earnest* by Oscar Wilde.

- Reading guide – *The Picture of Dorian Gray* by Oscar Wilde.

www.brightsummaries.com

Ebook EAN: 9782808017107

Paperback EAN: 9782808017114

Legal Deposit: D/2019/12603/22

Cover: © Primento

Digital conception by Primento, the digital partner of publishers.